Copyright Material

This book or parts thereof may not be reproduced in any form whatsoever, store or transmitted by any means-electronic, photocopy, mechanical recording or otherwise without prior permission of the publisher.

Copyright @2019 by Mike Smiths

All right reserved

Table of Contents

Amazon Echo overview   3

The Amazon Echo Devices Line-up   3

What Amazon Echo can do?   7

Using Echo for entertainment   8

Using Echo for productivity   8

Amazon Echo and smart home   9

What you get out of Echo   9

Some important Alexa commands   13

Alexa for kid   20

Alexa Bluetooth set-up   22

How to set-up Amazon Echo Auto   25

Setting up Echo Dot 3rd Generation: Manual wifi set-up   27

Using Echo as Bluetooth speaker   30

Amazon Echo overview:

Amazon artificial intelligent assistant what's it all about?

Amazon Echo is a small smartly designed speaker that does more than just playing music for you. It is a device that is useful in so many ways e.g. it can create a shopping lists, tell you about the weather, control your other smart devices like TV, lights, doors etc.

The Echo Auto basically has 8 smart microphones to listen to the "Alexa" keyword; the microphone is so smart and powerful that it can pick up voice commands over surrounding noise in the environment. This virtual assistant is also portable and can carry across many vehicles.

The Amazon Echo Devices line-up

Echo was originally launched by Amazon in 2015 as a smart device. Though, the originality of the concept for a smart home did not started with Amazon's Echo device, but they have greatly pushed the idea of speaking with your devices to a popular trend that's in vogue today. Four years after the initial introduction of this gadget, Amazon's Echo line now includes;

- Echo (2nd Generation)
- Echo Dot (3rd Generation)
- Echo Plus (2nd Generation)
- Echo Input
- Echo Show (2nd Generation)
- Echo Spot
- Echo Look

Echo (2nd Generation)

This is particular devices is only about 5.8 inch tall, smarter and smaller than its predecessor. It comes with a Dolby speaker which is a state of the art, couple with strong voice recognition feature. It can control over hundreds of connected devices at a go. It also has the ability to make calls and playback streaming from your devices. It allows you take control of your home gadgets without the use of remote.

This virtual assistant requires WI-FI connection to function effectively. Once it is set up, you train Alexa to recognize your voice. This technology is so sensitive that it can hear and recognize your voice, even at the peak of noise in your environment. It comes with seven multi- directional microphones with noise's cancellation ability. This

Echo becomes better with continue use and it requires minimal maintenance.

Echo Dot (3rd Generation)

Amazon Echo Dot 3rd generation device makes a debut into the market in 2016. This technology has a better speaker output, about 70% better than the previous version. With Alexa voice control, it does everything you want, like telling Alexa to increase the volume of TV or to increase the brightness of light. You can actually use this technology as your primary Echo device.

Echo plus (2nd Generation)

This technology comes in two formats, as a standalone or as a bundle device. It is packed with a great sound quality speaker aided by Dolby 360 degree sound. It can easily control over 400 smart devices at home with the aid of an in-built Zigbee smart hub. It also comes with a temperature sensor that detects room temperature. Moreover, it allows you to regulate the temperature appropriately through a command.

Echo Input

The Amazon family of Echo products grows further with the introduction of Echo input device. This virtual assistant comes with a huge library of skills including a better voice. The product weigh less than 3 ounces and can be taught over 50,000 skills including games, TV streaming, weather readout, kindle audio book reading and much more. Input can connect your speaker through a Bluetooth or aux cable and can be completed by pairing your WI-FI with Alexa app and to the system.

Echo Show (2nd Generation)

This virtual assistant is a hybrid of Amazon Echo and tiny TV. It can perform most of any Echo's task. The device is about 10.1 inch in size and the screen is about 1080p HD screen. More features are expected to be added to this device. The current features include: ability to place video calls, set a timer/reminder, streaming of live TV, reading audio book and much more.

Echo Spot

This devices is powered by the cloud based Alexa App just like other Echo devices. It's weigh 14.8 ounce and has 2.5 inch screen size with updated long distance voice recognition ability. This technology is highly compatible with Fire OS, IOS and Android devices. It sync with other Echo smart devices once connected to your home WI-FI. It allows you access to news, play music, regulates your thermostats, makes calls and much more. The device can connected to external speakers through cable or Bluetooth.

Echo Look

This virtual assistant is simply amazing with all what it can do. Little wonder, it is often refers to as a "connected fashion consultant". This device is great for fashion-conscious users as it can give an advice on what to wear or what not to wear through a feature called "style check". Echo look also comes with the standard options available in other Echo devices; news, traffic, music, weather etc. Its magic lies in the in-built 5 magapixel with intel RealSense SR300 high technology based camera that are compatible with IOS and Android.

What Amazon Echo can do?

Echo can do virtually all you ask her to do. It is like you are talking to a real person as she has response to virtually whatever you said. Echo also has an app for Apple and Android. This app enables you to take control of your Echo and perform many activities at a go. Echo is good at performing activities like:

- Managing your calendar appointment
- Add items to your shopping lists.

- Make your phone calls.
- Play music
- Read audio books
- Check reminder
- Find locations
- Etc

Using an Echo for Entertainment

Entertainment is part of the major use for this technology. We ask alexa to play one of our favorite radio stations or if we have a subscription to prime music, we can ask for any music listed for any artist. Aside this, Echo can also be use to read your kindle books, play games, tell jokes and much more.

Using Echo for Productivity

Entertainment aside, Echo can also serve as a primary source of information on the traffic situations, weather, sports update and news. If you tell Echo the details of your program for the day, it can give you an insight into specific traffic and weather related issues you may likely experience for the day. This technology can also help you make a shopping lists that you can access and edit through your Smartphone app. It can as well handle service like Evernote and Google calendar to keep your record of to-do lists.

Some other functionality skills you can add to your Echo include the function that allows you request for Uber without touching your phone. Some others are those that allow you place order for pizza, dictate messages and the one that tells you the best pairing wine that go with your meal.

Amazon Echo and the Smart Home

Are you ready to get onboard to use this technology? The good news is that this virtual assistant can actually be use to control virtually anything in your home. As a control hub connected to other smart devices, your home is practically in your hands. Though some smart home devices require an additional hub to function but this not an issue to worry about as the app include a list of compatible devices and the skills required of them.

WHAT YOU GET OUT OF ECHO

There are pretty much this smart device can do -- so much that it can be difficult to know where to start. Below are some of the features you can get out of this wonderful app.

1. It can be use to make phone calls (majorly, landline calls).

We might be thinking of the end for house phones, Amazon has resuscitated this. It is good to know that Alexa can perform the function of house phone by making calls to other houses that have Alexa device. This device also allows you to leave a message just like the answering machine we used to have around in the 90s. Thus, you can receive call from anyone who has your number. Another edge of this technology is its feature that allows you to do away with unwanted incoming calls by blocking them.

2. It can be use to control your smart home

Alexa is pretty good at performing some smart home tasks; like controlling your gadgets and appliances, door, locks, lights, switches and many other smart home tasks. You can check up for more of the smart home compatibility tool to know more of what Alexa works best with. Below are few of them:

- To control your light:

    You can command Alexa to turn on or off the lights and change the light color if the lights are color-changing.

- To control the garage door:

    You can also tell Alexa to close or open the door of your garage.

- To regulates the temperature:

You can as well use Alexa to regulate the temperature. "Hey Alexa, set the temperature to 55." Some of the thermostats that are compatible with Alexa on this technology are Nest, Ecobee and Honeywell.

3. It can be use to get cooking tips:

Though Alexa cannot cook the actual food but it makes cooking less stressful and easier for you. Alexa can be a kitchen assistant in the areas like:

- Getting conversions. "Alexa, tell me the number of tablespoons of sugar in a half-cup?"

- Asking for various recipes. Alexa can assist you in getting recipes especially from AllRecipes. Alexa can also be used to follow recipes step-by-step on your iPadwith GoodNes.

- Playing music. "Hey Alexa, play some cool country music."

- As a timer. You can set multiple timers and ask for the time remaining to plan your activities.

4. Getting regular news

Alexa allows you to get news from news sources you like to get news from, this is referred to as flash briefing and can be customized to suit you. Alexa can let you know what is happening in the world.

5. It can be use to entertain kids.

Alexa is kids friendly with loads of games that keep your kids busy and entertained. Games and activities like Easter eggs, funny answers to funny questions, set timers, play music and lots more.

6. It can be use to learn about more features.

There is a special feature on Alexa called a Skill Finder which can be use to find new skills. You can launch by saying the command "Alexa, open kill finder and give me the skill of the day."

7. It can be use to keep fit

Alexa can do this by giving you fitness feedback and guidance. Alexa can help you keep fit in the following ways:

- To check your FitBit statstics. You can ask Alexa by saying, "Alexa, ask FitBit how I'm doing right now."

- To get nutrition information by saying "Alexa, how many calories in a banana?"

- To do a workout. This can be done after enabling the 5 Minute Workout skill, by just saying, "Alexa, Start 5 Minute Workout."

8. It can be use to Control your TV

Alexa can save you the trouble of having to be looking everywhere for your remote. Alexa allow you to control your TV entirely by voice and command it by words like:

- Alexa, turn on the TV.

- Alexa, turn down the volume of the TV.
- Alexa, increase the brightness of the TV.
- Alexa, turn on Netflix.

You will need a Longitech Harmony remote to easily do this. This mostly comes with the Harmony Hub.

9. It can use Spotify to play music

The Alexa default music player is Amazon music, but this setting can be change to spotify. There are many built-in features for Amazon music and you can control this by saying something like "Alexa, play the song of the day"

10. You can train Alexa to do practically anything

Presently, it is practically impossible for Alexa to talk to or recognize every device because many companies have not gotten on board yet. At the same time, not all features of supported devices are controllable by Alexa. This little problem can be overcome by using IFTTT. You integrate some of the function through IFTTT programming. For instance, you can use IFTTT to create a "rule" that changes your light bulbs' to your desired color when your timer is well set up.

Some important Alexa commands

Alexa music's command

"Alexa, play music [genre]"

"Alexa, play country music from my [music service]."

"Alexa, play the latest James Brown"

"Alexa, play country music"

"Alexa, who sings this song?"

"Alexa, pair my Iphone"

"Alexa, louder"

''Alexa, slower''

"Alexa, increase the volume to 5"

"Alexa, switch it off in 3 minutes"

"Alexa, create a jazz playlist."

"Alexa, play life by J.Blake from the Bedroom TV."

<u>How to use Alexa EQ controls</u>

"Alexa, set the treble to four"

"Alexa, cancel night mode"

"Alexa, decrease bass."

"Alexa, increase treble."

"Alexa, increase bass in bedroom room."

"Alexa, set night mode on sitting room TV."

"Alexa, set movie mode."

"Alexa, set bass to four on sound bar."

Alexa movie/TV commands

"Alexa, what is the IMDb rating for [show/movie]?"

"Alexa, tell me about the movie [whatever it's called]"

"Alexa, who stars in [show/movie]?"

Alexa Fire TV commands

"Alexa, watch [title]"

"Alexa, open Netflix"

"Alexa, pause."

"Alexa, Play"

"Alexa, fast forward 2 minutes"

"Alexa, next / next Episode."

"Alexa, turn down volume on Fire TV."

"Alexa, show me movies with [actor's name]"

Alexa timers and alarm commands

"Alexa, start alarm by 4am"

"Alexa, wake me up at 4am to [TV station]."

"Alexa, snooze the alarm after ringing for ten seconds"

"Alexa, set timer for 2 minutes."

"Alexa, set a 12 minute breakfast timer."

"Alexa, tell me the time left on the timer?"

"Alexa, halt the timer"

Checking calendars and reminders

"Alexa, what is on my schedule today?"

"Alexa, add 'pizza at Mike's house' to my calendar for Sunday"

"Alexa, add features meeting to my calendar on Monday at 2.00pm"

"Alexa, what have I got on today?"

"Alexa, add pedicure cut to my to-do list"

"Alexa, what is on my to-do list today?"

Getting everyday information

"Alexa, what's the weather like?"

"Alexa, will it rain heavily today?"

"Alexa, what will the weather be like next week Monday?"

"Alexa, what's in the news today?"

"Alexa, what's the traffic like this morning?"

"Alexa, what time is it in Arizona?"

"Alexa, what movies are playing?"

"Alexa, what's yesterday's Liverpool match score?"

"Alexa, when is the Arsenal game?"

Controlling your smart home

The functionality of this command will depend on the presence of Alexa compatible smart home device in your household. Try these commands:

"Alexa, discover my devices". [To find smart home tech]

"Alexa, turn my table lights on"

"Alexa, bedroom lights off/out"

"Alexa, dim the sitting room lights to 50%"

"Alexa, set the dining light to blue."

"Alexa, set the room temperature to 24 degrees"

"Alexa, start the Purple Rain recipe"

"Alexa, close the rear door"

"Alexa, switch on the sitting room TV"

Making and taking calls

"Alexa, call Johnson"

"Alexa, answer that call"

"Alexa, end the call"

"Alexa, play my messages"

"Alexa, announce that [message]" – plays on all home network Echo devices.

Shopping

"Alexa, buy more [Amazon item]."

"Alexa, order [Amazon item]"

"Alexa, what's on my shopping list?"

"Alexa, add pizza to my shopping list"

"Alexa, where's my stuff?" [to track order]

The top Alexa's Ambient commands

"Alexa, start bedtime routine"

"Alexa, show me front camera.

"Alexa, play that song that ends with love."

"Alexa, how can I make smoothie recipe?"

"Alexa, how does (word) spelt?"

"Alexa, switch my accounts"

"Alexa, open Domino's skill" [to enable a skill for the first time]

"Alexa, sing me a R&B song"

"Alexa, make a cat noise"

"Alexa, pair my Iphone"

ALEXA FOR KIDS

Your kids can actually make friend with Alexa as she help them to grow in their daily learning activities. Alexa can stimulate and actually increase your kids learning rate as well as increase their intelligent quotient's level. There are many skills specifically made for kids on Alexa, and it's no surprise that some first word could actually be "Alexa". The List of things Your Kids can ask Amazon Alexa is endless. Here are few Alexa skills for kids.

"Alexa, play [name of podcast] podcast"

The family can be entertained with kid's tales and entertaining news by asking Alexa to play a podcast through the echo device with a built-in radio app to listen to their favorite podcasts. You can also play a specific episode by adding such skill as Stictcher or Anypod. Here are some other skills you can find in Alexa for kids:

"Alexa, where can I find Santa?"

Kids can use this command to track Santa location with the help of the NORAD Santa Tracker skill for Alexa.

"Alexa, open the Amazon Story time book."

This command will open the Amazon professional narrated story book for kids. This skill is helpful if you want the kids to sit and relax for few minutes.

"Alexa, start the Kids Court."

This skill can be use to settle kids argument. The Alexa kids Court's skill creates a courtroom situation where kids argue their case within the U.S judicial structure system. The cases are judge in a fair manner.

"Alexa, ask Funny things, tell me to do Funny thing."

This skill will certainly keep your kids amuse all the time.

"Alexa, roar like a lion."

If your kids are the restless types, the roar of a lion will startled them for few seconds. You can as well ask Alexa to make different animals sound e.g. monkey, cow, cat, bear, hippopotamus, baboon, rooster etc.

"Alexa, sing 'Happy Birthday for me."

Alexa can sing you happy birthday song with a wondrous skill. Take note, you might hear Alexa sing this song at odd time once our kids discover that Alexa can do this.

"Alexa, start the spelling game."

This skill will sharpen the spelling skill of your kids and prepared them for a real life spelling challenge.

"Alexa, tell me a joke."

This skill will even make your kids to love interacting more with Alexa. Listening to funny jokes will lighten their mod.

ALEXA BLUETOOTH SETUP: Mobile Device Pairing with Amazon Echo

Are you using Bluetooth to connect your mobile device to your echo or using Bluetooth to connect your echo to an external speaker? Amazon echo can be used as an external speaker for your devices using Bluetooth or it can be connected to an external speaker. So if you do have a speaker that you would rather use instead and have all the functionality of your echo. You can connect it up using Bluetooth. The process of achieving this is really easy.

We will start by connecting a mobile phone to the Echo. In this case let use an iPhone as an example because I am an Apple user and I don't have an Android so the first thing we are going to do is to enter settings mode, then go to your Bluetooth and now you're ready. To Pair a device to the phone, you'll go to your Echo and say computer enter pairing searching. Check the device you'd like to use and make sure Bluetooth is turned on. To set up a new device, go to your Alexa app now that said "pairing" even though

Its gave me that whole warning it shows up in Bluetooth of the Echo that I want to

Connect to. So I'll select that Echo "connected to smiths mike syns iPhone". Now that you're paired, next time just say connect my phone and there she go immediately. So that's what you need to do and next times you'll just need to say connect your phone and it'll be connected. Right up, you have multiple devices or phones it will connect to the one that you were most recently connected to and if we want a different one we just need to specify which device you'd like to connect to. Now that we're connected we can go to our phone and play some music.

One important thing we must note is that, after setting up Amazon Echo as a Bluetooth speaker, you cannot take phone calls on your Echo, so you can't use it as a wireless or as a Bluetooth speaker to have conversations and you're not going to get your text alerts on here.

If you want to connect to a laptop or another device, you would go through the same process. You would say the command "computer interfering" and then go to device you're already connected to.

 Now that the devise have been paired. Next time just say connect my phon. isn't that look great and easy? That was how to play some music from our laptop. Now I have gotten two devices hooked up, we have connected a mobile device and we've connected a laptop to use this as an external speaker, but let's say we want to connect this external speaker to the Echo so that we can move it around and still be able to listen to our Echo. To do that, we have to use the Alexa app for this. So we will open up our Alexa app and go to the upper left-hand corner to the three low lines. Open up the settings and then you'll want to select the device that we're using the office Echo. Here we will select that, then select Bluetooth and there chose the items that we have already paired up. Then we can pair a new device and it's going to be searching and so far it's picked up a couple of things that it sees flowing around that have Bluetooth signals. For example, if my Apple TV is on, it will detect and recognize it easily. After the detection by the device, then we are going to enter the pairing mode. While in pairing mode, we will wait for mini jambox pad to pop up and when this happened, it means we have successfully paired the devices. So, next time just say connect to my speaker now. I could request music from my Echo and it's going to play through my Bluetooth speaker. So for example, ''Computer plays some classical music''. Classical music commands on music immediately. So if I wanted to head out into the garage, I can simply pause the music with a command. This will trigger a pause function on the device.

To disconnect, I would simply say "computer disconnect''. Speaker now disconnected from CPU gen box'' that's basically pretty simple process. Now I can easily toggle between my devices just by using my voice. I can say computer, ''Connect a speaker'', "Computer play classical music''. "Computer connect to Smiths Mike's macbook'' and all these would be done in a twinkle of an eye.

HOW TO SET UP AMAZON ECHO AUTO

Set up your Echo auto when it is safe to do so. To successfully set up echo Auto, the following are needed:

- The Alexa app. (This you can install on your smart phone).
- A car stereo supporting Bluetooth (not less than 4.0 versions)
- A power adapter.
- A micro USB cable
- A USB port plug-in device.

You can as well make use of a built in USB port if you can get any available. To get the process started, turn on your car and switch on the Bluetooth on your phone set, your car stereo to Bluetooth or aux depending on your connection type. Ensure your car stereo support the Bluetooth music streaming but if it doesn't, you can use the included auxiliary cable to connect the device to your stereo. To complete this process of setting up the device in the Alexa app, choose the devices icon and thereafter, the plus sign then choose, add device.

Next step is to choose Amazon Echo and lastly Echo Auto. From there, you can follow the instructions to complete the set up process. Please note that some permissions including access to your location and microphone are required to complete setup, depending on your Smartphone and car types.

If you're having issues setting up Echo Auto with your Smartphone, then try these

Steps:

- Disconnect the cable from power source for 40 seconds and plug it back.
- Look out for an orange light in the device, if the light doesn't come up, then press down the action button for six to ten seconds to put the device in setup mode.
- Patiently go through the device setup steps once again.
- You can also pair echo Auto with a second user by pressing down the action button for about 10 seconds to trigger the pairing mode feature.
- Then go through the setup steps again.

You can use the included - mount to place Echo Auto in your car. Use a little alcohol with a cleaning pad to clean the dashboard surface and thereafter peel the plastic covers off the - mount position of the device, so as to allow the LED light bar to face you. Echo Auto can be left plugged in when you're not driving but it is better to unplug the in-car power adapter if the car is not going to be used for a long period of time.

Depending on your car, you may have to customize Echo Auto to allow Alexa to hear you better. You can do this by changing the response time for Alexa.

For Echo Auto set up.

- Go to devices
- Then all devices
- Echo Auto and
- Scroll down to advanced settings to adjust the response time. The value for the setting that works best is 500 milliseconds

SETTING UP ECHO DOT 3RD GENERATION: MANUAL WIFI SETUP

This process will walk you through the steps of how to set up your Amazon echo dot third-generation manually. Plug in your echo dot and wait for Alexa to say hello. This is actually a pretty straightforward process with steps one and two being the most important.

Step One:

Take out your power adapter and plug one side in to the wall and then plug in the power cord to the back of the device. A blue light will come up and begin to blink at the top of the device and in few minute, Alexa will come alive with greetings and thereafter direct you on how to complete the setup process with the Alexa app. You must use the items included in the original box for optimal performance.

I can tell you that the speaker on this generation of echo dot is much better than the second generation.

Step Two:

We're going to download the Alexa app. It says download the latest version of the Alexa app from the App Store. The app helps you get more out of your echo device, it's where you set up calling and messages, manage music lists settings, news and other features.

If you are not prompted to set up your device after you open your Alexa app, tap the device's icon in the lower right corner of the Alexa app to get started. To download Alexa app and set up your new echo device on your phone is pretty easy. If you are using Android, go to the Google Play Store and if you're on an Apple device then go to the app store and launch it. After this, go ahead and search for Amazon Alexa, click on it and installed the application.

You can open it right there in the Google Play Store or you can just find the little icon on one of your either home page or other pages on your Smartphone device and launch Amazon Alexa. If you had already download the application previously, it will not required you to log in but if this is your first time You need to have to log into your Amazon account to go to the next step and then you're going to be adding your Echo. So in the bottom right hand corner we're going to click that little house icon and then click Echo and Alexa and after this, click my one Amazon device that's not currently online and that's the one named Echo dot third-generation and yours is probably going to be named at something different probably your first name (followed by Echo Dot or Echo Auto) and then Wi-Fi network we're going to click Change and begin Echo setup. Now we're going to go ahead and click continue and then it says obviously plug your Echo into the power outlet. After about a minute .when the light turns from blue to orange, tap continue. After you must have tapped continue, it will ask you to manually connect to it now. Go to Wi-Fi settings in your phone and connect your phone to Amazon device as its display on your phone screen. This might be a combination of different letters and numbers.

Thereafter, go into your settings, in my own case it says Amazon at TFN open (yours will be different) .So I'm going to click that and then click connect. You are connected; now go back to the Alexa app.

It will says, continue Echo set ups, click continue and then it will ask which Wi-Fi network you want to set up which is obviously going to be different for you than me mine's called frontier 24 and then please wait while it connect your Echo to the internet, this may take a few minutes to complete. After successful completion, your device is ready for use. We are going ahead to clicks continue. After you go through that setup process you should be hooked in to the internet and your device should be ready for use.

USING ECHO AS BLUETOOTH SPEAKER

Your Echo can be use as a Bluetooth speaker; this is pretty easy to set-up.

Which is just say hey Alexa turn on bluetooth pairing and then put on your phone. You are to swipe down and go ahead and turn on Bluetooth and then tell it to search. Here it is Echo hood tap on that we are going to use.

Tell her next time connects my phone and you automatically pair. We can do all kind of things like listening to music; you can even have your like in YouTube as well which I think is really cool.

So,if you really like, you can watch your videos and hear the sound through your Echo or play music or whatever. It'll all work good and when you are done just say Alexa disconnects Bluetooth now. Disconnect it from lgk twenty-plus there it is and just that easy you're paired.

I think the Echo Auto is so great that it allows you the flexibility of innovating with great ideas.

www.ingramcontent.com/pod-product-compliance
Lightning Source LLC
Chambersburg PA
CBHW080605060326
40689CB00021B/4947